THE MANLY ART OF COLORING

THE MANLY ART OF COLORING

35 SPECTACULAR SCENES OF MASCULINE HUBRIS

Illustrations by
FÁBIO LYRA

callisto
publishing
an imprint of Sourcebooks

Published by Callisto Publishing LLC C/O Sourcebooks LLC

P.O. Box 4410, Naperville, Illinois 60567-4410

(630) 961-3900

callistopublishing.com

Printed and bound in the United States of America.

PAH 10 9 8 7 6 5 4 3 2 1

INTRODUCTION

It's been a long day of grueling work—breaking wild horses, drilling ice cores in Antarctica, sending emails—and it's time to relish the day's labors. Enter *The Manly Art of Coloring*. Now you can relax and let your creativity reign as you color in scenes of men just like you: gentlemen who tackle every task ahead of them with a "go big" mindset...no matter how that shakes out.

There's no right way to use this coloring book but your way. Particularly proud of one of your creations? Show it off! Hang it in your garage or on the fridge in your childhood home. Who cares if your parents don't live there anymore?

ART IS FOR EVERYONE.